T0165590

Little Books of Guidance
Finding answers to life's big questions!

Also in the series:
What Do We Mean by 'God'? by Keith Ward
How Do I Pray? by John Pritchard
What Does It Mean to Be Holy Whole? by Timothy F. Sedgwick
How to Be a Disciple and Digital by Karekin M. Yarian
What Is Christianity? by Rowan Williams
Who Was Jesus? by James D. G. Dunn
Why Go to Church? by C. K. Robertson
How Can Anyone Read the Bible? by L. William Countryman
What Happens When We Die? by Thomas G. Long
What About Sex? by Tobias Stanislas Haller, BSG

WHY SUFFERING?

A Little Book of Guidance

IAN S. MARKHAM

Church Publishing
NEW YORK

Unless otherwise noted, the Scripture quotations contained herein are from the New Revised Standard Version Bible, copyright © 1989 by the Division of Christian Education of the National Council of Churches of Christ in the U.S.A. Used by permission. All rights reserved.

Church Publishing
19 East 34th Street
New York, NY 10016
www.churchpublishing.org

Cover design by Jennifer Kopec, 2Pug Design
Typeset by Progressive Publishing Services

Library of Congress Cataloging-in-Publication Data

A record of this book is available from the Library of Congress.

ISBN-13: 978-0-89869-190-0 (pbk.)
ISBN-13: 978-0-89869-191-7 (ebook)

Printed in the United States of America

Contents

Acknowledgments

I am grateful to Davis Perkins and Nancy Bryan, who urged me to write this book. The act of doing so became an important vehicle of meditation for me on the cosmic themes of God and suffering. I am grateful to friends and colleagues that give me the space to write, especially my senior team—Melody Knowles, Jacqui Ballou, Barney Hawkins, Katie Glover, and Jim Mathes. And as always, I am grateful to Katherine Malloy, who keeps my life in order.

In writing a book on suffering, I am reminded afresh of my many blessings. And, as always, I am grateful to my wife Lesley and my son Luke for being my companions on this journey of life.

Ian S. Markham

About the Author

Ian S. Markham is Dean and President of Virginia Theological Seminary, Alexandria, Virginia, and author of more than a dozen books. Included among his publications are *Faith Rules; Episcopal Questions, Episcopal Answers;* and *Liturgical Life Principles*—all from Morehouse Publishing. He is Priest Associate at St. Paul's Episcopal Church in Alexandria.

Introduction

Perhaps some of the hardest moments to be a Christian is when you are watching the news on television. Every single day we learn of lives that are lost, leaving families and friends who are hurting. The hurricane that leaves a trail of devastation and death. The civil war that creates numerous victims—fathers and brothers killed, women and children turned into refugees. Less dramatically, on a typical day in the United States, there are 104 deaths due to car accidents.[1] With each death, loved ones mourn, and the outward ripples from such tragedy can be enormous. With the loss of a sibling, spouse, friend, child, or parent, other lives can descend into pain and anguish, and divorce and alcoholism can follow. Suffering is an intrinsic part of being human.

But why? Why is there suffering? This book will explore this hard and difficult question. It is one that must be treated with deep respect. There will be moments when the only answer is

---

[1] See the National Safety Council statistics for 2015. Accessed May 21, 2017. http://www.nsc.org/Connect/NSCNewsReleases/Lists/Posts/Post.aspx?List=1f2e4535-5dc3-45d6-b190-9b49c7229931&ID=103&var=h ppress&Web=36d1832e-7bc3-4029-98a1-317c5cd5c625.

that there is no good answer. Barney Hawkins, a priest with many years of experience, captures that feeling when he writes:

> In Hickory, I presided at the funeral of a baby who died at four months of age. I got through the service by pure grit. At the graveside, after most of the mourners had departed, I stood helpless and overcome with emotion. Yes, I knew that "we are the Lord's," but in a brief moment I questioned it all. How could it be that a loving God would allow such sadness, such loss? Is there a God after all? Living one's priesthood is never without doubts and the loneliness of the dark.[2]

In tackling this question, we are on sacred ground. We need to tread carefully and reverently. We are forbidden to be glib or cavalier or complacent. This is hard work.

Therefore this book starts by exploring the problem in more detail. Some of this is fairly technical; it draws on debates within the philosophy of religion realm to identify the problem with some precision. For someone who is struggling intellectually with the problem of suffering, this is important. Other readers (perhaps those who are trying to cope with suffering) might want to skip this section. One can do so and still understand the subsequent chapters. In the second chapter, we will examine some of the classical responses to the problem, including the free will defense and the greater good defense. These are called "theodicies" (attempts to justify why God allows suffering).

And then in the third chapter, we will look more closely at the Christian claim that in Jesus Christ we can see God and the enormous significance of God dying on a cross on Good Friday. As the

---

[2] Barney Hawkins, *Episcopal Etiquette & Ethics: Living the Craft of Priesthood in the Episcopal Church* (New York: Morehouse Publishing, 2012), 75–76.

chapter headings reveal, the second chapter provides the "head answers"—those answers that try to provide some sort of rational response. In the third chapter, we will hear from the responses of the heart—the response that makes us see that although understanding precisely why God allows suffering is hard, Christians do believe in a God that enters into suffering and seeks to redeem it.

In the fourth chapter, we move out from Good Friday and look at the rest of the Christian narrative. The doctrine of the Fall helps us understand our own propensities to inflict hurt on others, the doctrine of the atonement helps us to see that God wants to provide the resources for transformed living, the doctrine of the Church helps us see how we are called as persons redeemed by Christ to alleviate suffering, and the doctrine of the resurrection helps us understand how ultimately God redeems all suffering. And in the last chapter, we will look at ways in which Christian tradition teaches us how to cope with suffering. Three areas will be explored: gratitude, worry, and trust. The book ends by emphasizing that although we might only have clues as to why God allows suffering, we do have resources, provided by God, that help us cope with suffering.

1

The Problem

There is a sense in which the problem of suffering is obvious. God, according to the Christian tradition, is perfect love and absolute power. On the human level, no loving parent wants to see children suffer, so on the divine level, a being of perfect love must want to eliminate suffering. Given that this being is absolute power, this being must be able to eliminate suffering. So we arrive at the problem of suffering. Why does a being of perfect love and absolute power allow suffering?

Although the problem on one level is obvious, let us explore some of the complexities, which can be grouped into two types. The first type is the range of forms that suffering can take, and the second type is why precisely suffering is a challenge to faith.

The forms of suffering

Theologians have been thinking about the problem of suffering for centuries, and the following list of types of suffering has emerged. These are:

1 Suffering as a result of moral evil.
2 Group suffering.

3 Suffering caused by nature.
4 Animal suffering.
5 Demonic and Satanic suffering.

Let us look at each in turn.

The first is suffering that is a result of moral evil. This is the suffering that humans inflict on each other through their decisions to be unkind and cruel. This can be everything from the relatively trivial moments of driving inconsiderately, all the way up to the Holocaust. The death of six million Jews (and other victims) by a ruthless use of a state's military machinery is a classic illustration of the human capacity to inflict cruelty upon each other.

Although the Holocaust has many unique features, it is just one of many illustrations of systematic human cruelty. From the Rwandan Genocide of 1994 to the Bosnian Genocide of 1995, humans repeatedly allow and participate in horrendous crimes against each other. But it is important to stress that suffering through moral evil includes the countless acts of selfishness that we all perform every single day. These include the decision to be extravagant instead of giving to a person in need, the act of gossip, or the hurtful comment that we hurl in the middle of an argument to a spouse. All of this is covered under the first (and very large) category of suffering that is a result of moral evil. So the question arises: why does God allow us to inflict so much pain on each other?

The second type of suffering is a subsection of the first. This is suffering endured by particular groups. It is important to recognize that some groups suffer more than others. It was the African American philosopher, William R. Jones, who in a highly influential and provocative essay asked the question, is

God a white racist?[1] In the essay, he offers a critique of various classical theodicies of why African Americans have had to endure such a racist history. He finds all the theodicies implausible. Jones invites us to really live with the question: why does God allow particular groups to suffer so much more than other groups? If God is in control of history, why is it that some groups (such as the Jews or the African Americans) seem to have had such a disproportionately hard time?

The third type is suffering caused by nature. Nature might be beautiful, but it isn't sentimental. There is a brutality in nature. The calm ocean can easily turn wild; when it does so, lives can be lost in a major storm. Rain is a precious gift when it waters crops, but it can become treacherous when it becomes a flood. The wind is a natural process that moves clouds across the sky, but a hurricane can devastate entire towns. Nature is indiscriminate; it takes out the innocent as well as the guilty. A young child is as likely to be killed as an aging man who has led a sinful life. When it comes to suffering caused by nature, it looks like God is the primary agent. Although there is a connection between human agency and the climate, most forms of weather-related disasters (an earthquake, for example) are not due to human actions. So the question arises: why does God allow a child to be killed by a flood?

The fourth type is animal suffering. Now this is a subsection of the third type. The food chain is pretty brutal. Smaller animals suffer as they are eaten by larger animals. The whole process of

---

[1] See William R. Jones, "Theodicy and Methodology in Black Theology: A Critique of Washington, Cone and Cleage," reprinted in *Black Theology,* eds. James H. Cone and Gayraud S. Wilmore (Maryknoll, NY: Orbis Books, 1993), 141–152.

evolutionary history is parasitic on the emergence of countless species that then die out as they fail to adapt to the changing environment. If in some sense the goal of creation was the emergence of humanity, then the processes of evolution are a long, wasteful, and deeply painful route to the goal. Why does a God create natural structures that are so painful to so many sentient creatures?

The fifth and final type is the suffering caused by the devil and by demons. Now at this point, some Christians solve this problem by simply saying that such entities are implausible and unlikely to exist. However, demons are a major part of the Gospel narrative, which describes Jesus constantly "casting them out." So the obvious question is this: why does God allow these evil entities so much space in the world? It is especially puzzling when one remembers that according to Scripture, God will ultimately triumph over the devil. If this is the ultimate plan, then why doesn't God speed up the process and get rid of the devil and demons right now?

As one looks at all the different types of suffering, one can understand the atheist who stops right here. These questions are simply unanswerable. As Sam Harris puts it,

> The problem of vindicating an omnipotent and omniscient God in the face of evil (this is traditionally called the problem of theodicy) is insurmountable. Those who claim to have surmounted it, by recourse to notions of free will and other incoherencies, have merely heaped bad philosophy onto bad ethics. Surely there must come a time when we will acknowledge the obvious: theology is now little more than a branch of human ignorance. Indeed, it is ignorance with wings.[2]

---

[2] Sam Harris, *The End of Faith* (New York: W. W. Norton and Co., 2005), 173.

At this point, it is important to note that Christians should never be afraid of questions. God created us with minds that have the capacity to think, so we need to enter in and enjoy the questions. However, let us make the questions a little more complicated. Why precisely is suffering a problem to faith?

Digging down into the problem

Philosophers like to be very precise with language. They want to move from the obvious sense in which suffering is a problem of faith (the simple question of "Why does God allow this?") to the more precise. Now some background is necessary at this point. Coherence is very important when it comes to belief. It literally means that beliefs cohere together. They make sense; it is an option because one belief does not cancel another belief out. So for example, if I started talking about drawing a "square circle," then you would rightly be puzzled. How can you have a square circle? We all know what a square is—it is a shape with four equal sides and four equal angles. We also all know what a circle is—it is a shape with no sides and no angles. So how can you draw a shape with both sides and angles and simultaneously no sides and no angles? It doesn't make sense. One cannot even imagine what the shape would look like. It is, to use a philosopher's favorite term, self-contradictory.

For a belief to become an option, the belief must be at least coherent. There are lots of coherent beliefs that do not exist. For example, the idea of unicorn—a horse-type beast with a horn coming out of its forehead—is a coherent idea and one can imagine it being true, but it probably doesn't exist. It is not like a square circle, which is intrinsically self-contradictory. The idea of a funny sort of horse with a horn is no stranger than cats without tails (which do exist—there is an entire breed of Manx cats on the Isle of Man). The question with unicorns is not whether the idea is coherent, but whether there is any evidence that they exist.

Armed with this background, philosophers talk of the problem of suffering in two ways. The first way is to treat it as a coherency problem with belief. Christians believe in a God with a certain set of attributes—a God who is powerful and all loving. Is this type of God compatible with the reality of suffering in the world? As we have just seen, the philosopher Sam Harris thinks that it is not. He sees these two beliefs as being self-contradictory. The incoherence of a "square circle" is easy to see, but the incoherence with an all-powerful and all-loving God is less obvious. Alison Krauss, the blues singer, says of suffering "there must be a reason for it all." She goes on to sing that "hurtin' brings my heart to you."[3] Now Sam Harris cannot say that this is definitely false. Perhaps Alison Krauss is right: there are reasons for suffering, and among these reasons is the closeness that develops between a human and God. This is possible. And if it is possible, then incoherence cannot be proved. So much like the idea of the unicorn, the idea of a God who is all powerful and loving and a suffering world are not obviously contradictory.

The second way in which philosophers talk about the problem of suffering is still very present. The idea of the unicorn is coherent, but it is not obvious that these mythical creatures really exist. We would need evidence that they exist, but all the evidence tends to point against this. This is called the "evidential problem of

---

[3] Alison Krauss, "There is a Reason," Lyrics. Accessed July 24, 2017. http://www.azlyrics.com/lyrics/alisonkrauss/thereisareason.html

evil." Philosophers who talk in this way concede that it is logically possible (which is just another way of saying that the belief is coherent) that suffering is compatible with the existence of God, but they still think that suffering is good evidence against the existence of God. Although God might have some reason, it still feels more likely than not that suffering points to the random nature of the world, where stuff just happens because it does.

So now we have a sense of the problem. And it is good to sit here for a moment. Christians often rush to solve a problem without living with the problem for a while. This is a serious challenge to faith. We have seen how many different forms that suffering takes. It isn't simply our innate propensity to be cruel to each other; it includes earthquakes; racism; animal suffering; and, if they exist, suffering caused by the devil and demons. Alison Krauss does make the point that incoherence is impossible to prove (there might always be a reason for why God allows suffering), but we are still left with a massive puzzle. One can understand why a person watching the television news might find themselves thinking, "I just cannot believe that there is a good God in control of this world." It just doesn't make sense.

How are we going to respond to this challenge? This is our task in the rest of this book. We turn now to our head answers.

2

Head Answers

Suffering is hard. Explanations for suffering can easily sound shallow and painful. When they have just lost a loved one, no one wants to be told, "Well, look on the bright side, at least they are in a better place." Even if heaven exists, suffering is an agony all of its own. Sometimes the moment does not need explanation. One just needs to live with the pain and agony.

But Christians do want to say that there are reasons why God allows suffering in this universe. Two main perspectives have been offered. The first focuses on human freedom, and the other on the values that emerge from suffering. The former is called the "free will defense," and the latter is the "greater goods defense." We start with the free will defense.

Forms of the free will argument can be found in a variety of contexts, from the writings of Augustine of Hippo to the contemporary philosopher of religion Alvin Plantinga. This argument is part of virtually every attempt to explain why evil and suffering exists. It starts with the assumption that the goal of creation is to have creatures who are able to have a loving relationship with each other and with God. Love cannot be programmed or compelled. Although I am able to set my computer on start up to announce "I love you," I know that this is not true love. True loves requires freedom—a freedom to hurt, disagree, and hate. And love is precious precisely because true love includes this possibility. As every parent knows, one of the finest moments in the world is when a child turns to them and says, "I love you, Daddy and Mommy." It is precisely because a child has the capacity to dislike and hate that the sentence is so extraordinary. So the free will defense goes like this: God desires a creation where there is love. Love requires freedom. Given love is a desirable end, then freedom is a necessary condition. However, freedom entails the possibility of evil. This possibility was realized (and is realized every day) by humans exercising their freedom for evil ends. Ultimately, at the end of the age, by God's grace, humans will have learned to use their freedom for good. This is the promise of heaven. But for now, we live with the struggle in us all. Every day, we are choosing. Sometimes our better selves triumph, and we choose to act in ways that are generous, gentle, and kind. Sometimes our shadow side triumphs, and we gossip and behave in vindictive and sometimes cruel ways.

While the free will defense focuses on our behavior (moral evil), the Irenaean theodicy focuses on the context in which we are living. It was John Hick, in his rightly acclaimed classic *Evil and the God of Love*, who argues for an Irenaean, rather than Augustinian, theodicy. According to Augustine, we as humans are placed into a perfect setting that we spoil by sinning; for Irenaeus (c. 130 to 202 CE) we are placed into a challenging setting through which we move from the image of God (our fundamental nature as creatures of intelligence) to the likeness of God (the state where the human is perfected by the action

10

of the Holy Spirit). Hick explains the contrast between Augustine and Irenaeus in this way:

> There is . . . to be found in Irenaeus the outline of an approach to the problem of evil which stands in important respects in contrast to the Augustinian type of theodicy. Instead of a doctrine that man was created finitely perfect and then incomprehensively destroyed his own perfection and plunged into sin and misery, Irenaeus suggests that man was created as an imperfect, immature creature who was to undergo moral development and growth and finally be brought to the perfection intended for him by his Maker. Instead of the fall of Adam being presented, as in the Augustinian tradition, as an utterly malignant and catastrophic event, completely disrupting God's plan, Irenaeus pictures it as something that occurred in the childhood of the race, an understandable lapse due to weakness and immaturity rather than an adult crime full of malice and pregnant with perpetual guilt. And instead of the Augustinian view of life's trials as a divine punishment for Adam's sin, Irenaeus sees our world of mingled good and evil as a divinely appointed environment for man's development towards the perfection that represents the fulfillment of God's good purpose for him.[1]

With this contrast established, Hick then develops the Irenaean theodicy in an interesting and imaginative way. God desires a world that is a vale of soul-making—a setting in which we move from immaturity into maturity. The setting is a stable one in which humans can exercise their freedom and learn to interact with each other. There is an appropriate distance between us and God: God is not so overwhelmingly obvious that we would not dare to develop our character and autonomy. With the challenge of coping with tragedy and pain, we develop character. John Hick

---

[1] John Hick, *Evil and the God of Love* (London: Collins, 1968), 220–221.

is pointing to an experience which is, fortunately, often recognized by people who suffer. It arises when a person who is forced to cope with some tragedy (such as a divorce) and then in retrospect decides "it was all for the good." A person, for example, may lose their job and in a moment of despair discover resources "deep" inside to transform the situation.

One truth about being human is that often suffering is the vehicle that helps one more clearly see the true value of things around us. So we never express deep gratitude for good health until we are in danger of losing it. We never appreciate the love of parents until they are in danger of going. We spend too much time wishing we had the luxury car or the fabulous vacation and fail to appreciate the gift of a friend who keeps us company or running water that comes out of the tap. The truth about suffering is that it often takes suffering to start seeing things aright.

Yet these head answers can feel inadequate when one learns of a child who was tortured and abused. It feels inadequate to say that this suffering is the inevitable result of the misuse of human freedom and will prove helpful in clarifying one's underlying disposition about life. Indeed, it sounds almost cruel. Such a response feels almost immoral.

This sense of unease with "head answers" is captured in the widely discussed chapter of Fyodor Dostoyevsky's novel *The Brothers Karamazov*. This remarkable novel of three sons—Dmitry (an army officer), Ivan (the sceptic writer), and Alyosha (a novice)—provides remarkable insight into Dostoyevsky's Russia of 1870. In the chapter titled "Rebellion," two of the brothers, Ivan and Alyosha, meet at an inn, where the conversation turns to religion, love, and evil. Ivan explains to Alyosha why he finds faith so difficult. Ivan refers to the suffering of children, who are innocent and have not yet "eaten the apple."[2] In each case, it is tragic and moving: one illustration will suffice for our purposes.

> I've collected a great deal of facts about Russian children, Alyosha. A father and mother, "most respectable people of high social position, of good education and breeding," hated their little five-year-old daughter. . . . This poor five-year-old girl was subjected to every possible torture by those educated parents. They beat her, birched her, kicked her, without themselves knowing why, till her body was covered with bruises; at last they reached the height of refinement; they shut her up all night, in the cold and frost, in the privy and because she didn't ask to get up at night (as though a child of five, sleeping its angelic, sound sleep, could be trained at her age to ask for such a thing), they smeared her face with excrement and made her eat it, and it was her mother, her mother who made her! And that mother could sleep at night, hearing the groans of the poor child locked up in that vile place! Do you realize what it means when a little creature like that, who's quite unable to understand what is happening to her, beats her little aching chest in that vile place, in the dark and cold, with her tiny fist and weeps searing, unresentful and gentle tears to "dear, kind God" to protect her? Can you understand why all this absurd and horrible business is so necessary and has been brought to pass?[3]

The narrative culminates in Ivan's absolute refusal to accept that any "justification" is acceptable for such tragedy. The suffering of that five-year-old child is too high a price to pay for cosmic harmony beyond the grave or as a necessary condition for human freedom. Ivan finds creation morally obscene. He explains:

> "Besides, too high a price has been placed on harmony. We cannot afford to pay so much for admission. And therefore I hasten to return my ticket of admission. And indeed, if I am an honest man,

---

[2] Fyodor Dostoyevsky, *The Brothers Karamazov* (Harmondsworth: Penguin Books, 1958, reissued 1982), 283.

[3] Ibid., 282–283.

I'm bound to hand it back as soon as possible. This I am doing. It is not God that I do not accept Alyosha. I merely most respectfully return him the ticket."

"This is rebellion," Alyosha said softly, dropping his eyes.

"Rebellion? I'm sorry to hear you say that," Ivan said with feeling. "One can't go on living in a state of rebellion, and I want to live. Tell me frankly, I appeal to you—answer me: imagine that it is you yourself who are erecting the edifice of human destiny with the aim of making men happy in the end, of giving them peace and contentment at last, but that to do that it is absolutely necessary, and indeed quite inevitable, to torture to death only one tiny creature, the little girl who beat her breast with her little fist, and to found the edifice on her unavenged tears—would you consent to be the architect on those conditions? Tell me and do not lie!"

"No, I wouldn't," Alyosha said softly.[4]

For Ivan, the problem is not God (the idea of God might be possible), but the creation. Ivan rejects completely and categorically all attempts at a theodicy that says "to get human freedom or character evil is necessary": for Ivan the end of freedom or character building cannot justify the means of the suffering of children. Ivan rejects the cosmic experiment where such means are used to such ends: "It is not God that I do not accept Alyosha. I merely most respectfully return him the ticket."[5] Ivan wants out of this experiment: the values of the project are fundamentally immoral.

Ivan has been described as a "protest atheist." It is a protest that this world is not worthy of a good God. If Ivan was put in a position where he had to make the same decision as God—to allow a child to be abused by her parents for the sake of human

---

[4] Ibid., 287–288

[5] Ibid., 288.

freedom and happiness at the end of the age, then Ivan would have decided against creation. The price is just too high.

Ivan captures our sense of unease. I suspect the traditional theodicies have real insights, but it is still hard. There is still a sense of heart-wrenching tragedy that makes it almost blasphemous to believe them. Is God really calculating that character building is worth a tsunami? Was God's inactivity at Auschwitz really a decision to protect the virtue of human freedom and the right to exercise that freedom for wickedness? If a human being had the power to do something about a tsunami or Auschwitz and decided that inactivity was appropriate because it led to some desirable end, then we would judge that human being very harshly. So why are our expectations of God less than our expectations of each other?

It is interesting that there is no theodicy in the Bible. Although the Bible documents the entire range of human suffering, nowhere do we find the free will defense or an Irenaean theodicy. The book in the Bible that explores suffering in the most detail is the elegant poetry book of Job. Job, so the story goes, is tested by God. He loses everything. Job's friends—Eliphaz, Bildad, and Zophar— suggest the traditional theodicy: suffering is a result of sin. So Job must have sinned. Later Elihu stresses the way in which suffering can transform us. Finally, after extensive pleading, God delivers the answer out of the whirlwind. And it is an extraordinary answer: God asks Job various questions, all of which make clear that God is the creator and Job a mere puny entity within creation. God says:

> Where were you when I laid the foundation of the earth?
> Tell me, if you have understanding.
> Who determined its measurements – surely you know!
> Or who stretched the line upon it?
>
> Job 38:4–5

And on it goes. In a remarkable set of questions put by God to Job (which strangely neglects the creation of humanity), God makes the point that the Creator is not obliged to provide answers to the questions that people ask. Job responds:

> I know that you can do all things,
>   and that no purpose of yours can be thwarted.
>   "Who is this that hides counsel without knowledge?"
> Therefore I have uttered what I did not understand,
>   things too wonderful for me, which I did not know.
>   "Hear, and I will speak; I will question you; and you will
>   declare to me."
> I had heard of you by the hearing of the ear,
>   but now my eye sees you;
>   therefore I despise myself,
>   and repent in dust and ashes.
>
>   Job 42:1–7

Job repents of the temerity of daring to ask questions. It is almost as if the Biblical answer is that God is not going to explain why the innocent suffer. The Biblical witness agrees that there is innocent suffering; indeed the Biblical witness documents all forms of suffering from natural disasters to despicable acts of human evil. But we are not told precisely why this is so. Yet the Bible does have an answer. It is not a "head answer," but there is an answer. It is an answer that appeals to the heart. The narrative of Scripture, for a Christian, culminates in the tragedy of a young man, Jesus of Nazareth, dying at the hands of an occupying power in Israel. And this instance of innocent suffering (for he had done nothing wrong) Christians believe is the very incarnation of God. This response I am calling a "heart response."

3

Heart Responses

Let us try a thought exercise. It is the year 5000 CE. The survival of the planet is at stake; earth is running out of power resources to support the population. Thanks to various probes, we know that there are substances on Mars that could completely solve the global fuel problem forever. In addition, there are no viable alternatives. After extensive study, it is determined that the only way to get to Mars is for the expedition to undergo a cryonic preservation, where the body is frozen and then reawakened as the rocket gets nearer to Mars. The risks are significant. This is not a safe process. Everyone will be damaged in some way; for some it will be extremely severe and for others less so. Naturally no one wants to go. The organization responsible for this work, "Mars, Inc.," has to make a decision on who will go. Given it is not technically difficult work, the expectation is that prisoners who have committed various crimes would be compelled to go, but the leader of the organization steps forward. "No. I am not going to outsource this work to anyone—not to the poor nor the wicked." "Instead," she says, "I will go. Who would like to join me?"

The thought exercise is envisaging a situation where doing nothing is not an option and the result is transformative. However, the only way forward to this transformative outcome is full of suffering.

Now who is going to suffer? The temptation is to force those who are weakest to suffer, but the leader makes a morally commendable decision. She insists on fully participating in the necessary process of suffering and promises to be alongside everyone else who goes.

This is intended as a poor analogy for the Christian claim. The picture we need is not to imagine a God who designs this cruel system for certain obscure reasons, but instead a God who in some sense had no choice but to create (this is an interesting and theologically complex question—did God have a choice not to create?) and then decides to be right at the heart of the suffering. It is the latter God that we find in the witness of Scripture.

There is something amazing about the claim that God became human. God, after all, is the creator of this vast universe, with perhaps 225 billion galaxies, and it is this creator God who became a baby in a manger in Bethlehem. If you don't find yourself pausing and marveling at this idea, then you are probably not grasping its significance. It is amazing. Is it really true that God became human? Let us look at this in stages. First, we will consider what is involved in God becoming human, and then we will consider the evidence for whether Jesus really was the incarnation of God.

The idea of the Incarnation[1]

The idea that a human can be identical to God is puzzling. After all, a human is finite, is limited, has a physical body, is forgetful, and is often wicked, while God is the opposite—infinite, unlimited,

---

[1] Parts of what follow is significantly adapted from my book titled *Understanding Christian Doctrine* (Oxford: Wiley Blackwell, 2017).

spiritual, omniscient (all knowing), and perfectly good. So how could a person actually be God? It is important to note that this is more than the idea of a person simply "showing us God." This means that a person actually is God.

For some skeptics, the whole idea of the Incarnation is just nonsense. The problem for many people is that they are operating with Leibniz's Law of Identity (even if they don't realize that they are). In what is called the indiscernibility of identicals by philosophers, the idea is that in order for two things to be identical, they must have all properties in common. With God and Jesus, the problem is obvious: God is transcendent and omnipotent, while Jesus is finite and limited. It is clear that they cannot be identical. It is true that if this is your picture of "identical," then you cannot believe in the Incarnation.

However, there are other models of identity that are more flexible. One can arrive at a more dynamic model of identity if one thinks of the way in which a five-year-old child grows into a forty-year-old adult. If you look at a picture of me when I am five, then you will see a person who looks quite different from me (the five year old had more hair and was cuter). But there is a unique connection between the five-year-old me and the subsequent adult writing this book now. We are identical, despite our numerous differences, because there is a unique continuity that connects myself as a child with myself as an adult.

The doctrine of the Trinity helps us with the challenge of making sense of the Incarnation. It is not necessary for Christians to believe that all of God is incarnate in Christ. Although Jesus is "all God," it is not true that all of God is in Jesus. If we did believe that all of God is in Jesus, then we would have no one sustaining the universe when Jesus was dying on the cross. It is the second person of the Trinity who is present in Jesus. The second person of the Trinity is of course inseparable from the other members of the Godhead, but that does not preclude the possibility of talking about a distinctive aspect of God's being in Jesus. The doctrine of the Incarnation involves the Eternal Word (the revealing disclosing aspect of God) being completely and uniquely present in the life, death, and resurrection of Jesus. Jesus, then, is identical with God in this way: the Eternal Word completely permeates the humanity of Jesus. This is done not in a way that eradicates the humanity; rather, it uses humanity to disclose and reveal God.

So we get the idea of the Incarnation. But is there any evidence that it is true?

The evidence for the Incarnation

The idea of "God becoming human" is so amazing that it should not be a surprise that some scholars are skeptical about the evidence for the truth of the Incarnation. They point out that the idea of the Incarnation is only fully developed in the Gospel of John, which was probably written in 90 CE, some sixty years after the life of Jesus. They look at the other three Gospels and see a man who certainly believed that he was some kind of agent of the end of the world, but did not talk about himself in Incarnational terms. So they find themselves thinking that even if the idea of the Incarnation makes sense, there isn't any evidence that Jesus thought of himself as God.

There are two major problems with this picture. First, it is important to remember that Christianity was a martyrdom religion. All that talk in the synoptic Gospels (Matthew, Mark, and Luke) about "taking up your cross" was meant literally. Jesus was inviting people to become his disciples and promising them that it was more than likely that they would be killed for their faith. These were men and women who were persuaded of the significance of Jesus. If Jesus was just another failed apocalyptic prophet (i.e., a person describing the turbulent events that will usher in the end of the world), then why be so committed to the movement?

Second, it is important to remember when we read the Bible that the epistles of Paul were written before the Gospels. The epistles are clear that a devotion to Jesus had arisen that gave Jesus the same significance in worship as God. We have Larry Hurtado to thank for a major study on this devotion to Jesus in earliest Christianity. As one reads the New Testament, the affirmation "Jesus is Lord" pulsates throughout the text. So many passages are a celebration of Jesus (see for example, Col. 1:15–20, Acts 2:36, and Phil. 2:1–11). Hurtado shows that this devotion to Jesus did not emerge gradually, but rather exploded on to the scene. Hurtado writes:

> Christians were proclaiming and worshipping Jesus, indeed, living and dying for his sake, well before the doctrinal/creedal developments of the second century . . . Moreover, devotion to Jesus as divine erupted suddenly and quickly, not gradually and late, among first-century circles of followers. More specifically, the origins lie in Jewish Christian circles of the earliest years.[2]

The suddenness of this eruption, coupled with its Jewish monotheistic context, is clear evidence of the remarkable impact that the totality of Jesus' life, death, and resurrection had on the first Christians. Here we have Jews who believed in one God and yet, at considerable personal cost, wanted to pray to and worship Jesus.

---

[2] Larry W. Hurtado, *Lord Jesus Christ: Devotion to Jesus in Earliest Christianity* (Grand Rapids, MI: Eerdmans, 2003), 650.

The point is that we do not simply have a Jewish prophet who preached the imminent end of the world. This life provided his followers with clear expectations of behavior, a celebration of love, and a commitment to the outcast that subsequent generations felt was worthy of worship. This is the important seed that slowly grew into the doctrines of the Incarnation and Trinity. For a Jewish monotheist, you cannot worship two gods. If you are worshipping Jesus, then you must be worshipping the one God.

There is a reason why the Church took over three hundred years to sort this out; this is complicated stuff. But the Church got it right. It spotted what was happening. As we read the New Testament, we have sufficient clues to know that it took some time for Jesus to realize that in his mind there were two poles—a human pole and a divine pole. It is clear from the Gospels that Jesus was human: he wept, and he was sometimes hungry, tired, and exhausted by the crowds. It is also clear from the Gospels that Jesus knew he had a close relationship with God: he was intimate with his heavenly Father.

When you become a Christian you are identifying with those disciples in the first century who decided to give their all to Jesus. It is an act of trust in the witness of those disciples. One is not granted complete certainty that it is all true (one isn't actually granted that certainty in any arena of life), but there are countless good reasons for the act of trust. In fact, many really important decisions have a trust-like character. I married Lesley, my wife, at age 24. Was I completely certain that we could cope with and walk together through all the challenges of life? No, but I did have sufficient reasons to trust that we could. And later, when Lesley and I were blessed with our son Luke, we had to make a similar decision to trust. Were we completely certain that we could handle the demands of parenting? No. But we did trust that we could get it right as much as we could.

The act of trust in those early disciples is a perfectly appropriate response to what we are seeing in the Gospels. We are seeing a life that is identical with God. And in the words of Jesus (that are often so demanding) and the deeds of Jesus (which are often so gentle), one can see the nature of the God that created this vast universe.

So what sort of God? And what about suffering?

The earliest gospel is the Gospel of Mark. Each gospel captures a different aspect of the extraordinary impact and nature of the ministry of Jesus. And the Gospel of Mark is the one where suffering is front and central. It is an intriguing gospel. Initially, we have a Jesus pulsating with urgency and concern (the word "immediately" is used in the gospel forty times). Jesus seems to saying "the reign of God has arrived, the world has changed, and we need to get a move on."

The identity of Jesus is intriguing. The disciples seem to be dreadfully dim: they don't get anything at all. The only voices who correctly identify Jesus are demonic and divine voices. The demons yell out, and the Father speaks at the baptism and the transfiguration. But apart from that, humans are pretty quiet. The two exceptions are Peter's great confession, "You are the Messiah" (Mark 8:29), and the Roman centurion at the crucifixion, right at the end of the gospel.

The crucifixion in Mark is described with a brutal simplicity. In John, Jesus seems very much in control of events. But in Mark, Jesus is a victim. There is only one saying from the cross in Mark: it is the cry of despair. The text reads: "At three o'clock Jesus cried out with a loud voice, 'Eloi, Eloi, lema sabachthani?' which means, 'My God, my God, why have you forsaken me?'"(Mark 15:34). Jesus is invoking a psalm of lament (Ps. 22:1). Where is God at this moment of extraordinary suffering and betrayal?

It is worth pausing at this moment. The Christian claim is that Jesus is identical with God. This means that Jesus is God. The person hanging on the cross is God. God is the betrayed one; God is the tortured one; God is the hurting one; and God is the one crying in despair, wanting to know where God is.

Now we have arrived at a heart response to suffering. The Christian "answer" to suffering is not the head answers of the last chapter. The Christian "answer" is Good Friday. It is an answer that says this: you need to know that the Creator of the universe has been where you are. The Creator knows what it is to suffer. The Creator understands that despair. Again, we are being invited to trust. We are not granted the gift of seeing exactly why suffering is necessary, but we are invited to see that the Creator God who is responsible for this universe has tasted suffering and is involved in the hurt and pain of this universe.

Christians believe that the Incarnation is not simply a past description of some things that happened to Jesus and therefore God, but that everything in that life is revelatory of God. So as we meditate on Good Friday, we see a God who has not simply tasted the pain of living and life, but we have revealed a God who promises to be in every instance of pain, to be present in the cries, and to know the agony. On the cross, we should not just see God hanging there, but we should also see every child who has been beaten and raped; every person who has been murdered; every refugee; every person dying of cancer; every person coping daily with depression; and, in fact, every person who is suffering in every form.

The thought exercise at the beginning of this chapter has many limitations. But the idea here is this: when we think about God and suffering, we must eliminate the idea from our minds of the observer God. God is not sitting on the sidelines, watching the cruel universe play out. Instead, God is right in the middle. There is a story found in Elie Wiesel's famous book *Night*, which describes Wiesel's experiences of Auschwitz. He recounts an enforced walk past victims who were hung in the yard of the concentration camp.

> Then came the march past the victims. The two men were no longer alive. Their tongues were hanging out, swollen and bluish. But the third rope was still moving: the child, too light, was still breathing . . .
>
> And so he remained for more than half an hour, lingering between life and death, writhing before our eyes.
>
> And we were forced to look at him at close range. He was still alive when I passed him. His tongue was still red, his eyes not yet extinguished.
>
> Behind me, I heard the same man asking: "For God's sake, where is God?"
>
> And from within me, I heard a voice answer: "Where He is? This is where—hanging here from this gallows . . ."
>
> That night, the soup tasted of corpses.[3]

For Elie Wiesel, who was a Jew and did not believe in the Incarnation, this powerful story meant this: God can be found right at the heart of suffering. This sentiment is precisely what Christians want to affirm; although, unlike our Jewish friends, we do affirm that God was literally in Christ and therefore literally

---

[3] Elie Wiesel, *The Night Trilogy: Night, Dawn, and Day* (New York: Hill and Wang, 2008), 82–83.

suffered. The Christian response to suffering is simply this: God knows, God understands, and God is present. The Christian response to Ivan in *The Brothers Karamazov* is to point to the person hanging and dying on the cross who we believe was God. Theologically we learn from this that God knows what suffering is and that this is an inescapable part of the creation. It is not a head response; rather, it is a very powerful heart response.

4

Suffering in the Wider Christian Narrative

Over the last fifteen or so years, I have been very involved in Christian-Muslim dialogue. I have worked hard to appreciate the beauty and structure of Islam. From time to time, a Muslim will ask me this question: "You clearly understand Islam. You clearly appreciate Islam. So why are you not a Muslim?" And each time I reply, "I love Islam, yet I find its response to the total experience of suffering as inadequate. I need to know that God understands. And I need to be able to place the problem of suffering in a broader narrative that makes sense of this complex dimension of living."

We have examined the central response of Christianity to suffering as found in the mystery of a young Jewish man who was crucified on the cross. But there is more to the Christian response of suffering that helps us understand further *why suffering*. There are four areas: first, the Christian understanding of humanity; second, the doctrine of the atonement; third, the doctrine of the Church; and finally, our understanding of the life to come. Taken together, these four areas—coupled with the doctrine of the Incarnation explored in the previous chapter—create a powerful response to the challenge of suffering.

Let us start with the Christian view of humanity. As Christians, we are very aware that humans are capable of goodness and at other times are agents of wickedness. The theological explanation for this is grounded in the doctrines of the creation and the fall as described in Genesis 1–3. Our goodness is made possible by the fact we are all created in the image of God, and our propensities for wickedness arise due to our struggle for autonomy (traditionally called the "fall").

In Genesis 1:26, the text reads:

> Then God said, "Let us make humankind in our image, according to our likeness; and let them have dominion over the fish of the sea, and over the birds of the air, and over the cattle, and over all the wild animals of the earth, and over every creeping thing that creeps upon the earth."

This is the famous concept of the *Imago Dei* (the image of God). Now of course the image of God does not mean that God has arms and legs. For the church fathers, it means that humanity reflects the divine capacity for loving relationships. We are creatures that can give and receive love. And this is the cosmic project of creation. God embarked on the 13.7 billion year process of creation to enable complex creatures like us to emerge. And our challenge and invitation are to use the gift of every moment to learn how to focus on others through love and also (because often this is hard) to learn how to receive the focus from others through love. In Christian theology, it is the fact that we have the image of God that humanity has the remarkable capacity to be heroic, generous, and kind. In countless ways, every day, the image of God is seen in the regular dealings of a mother and child, a neighbor and a friend, and acts of kindness between strangers.

But Christianity believes that learning how to give and receive love is difficult. And this is where the doctrine of the Fall comes in. One misunderstands Genesis if you treat it like some past event, involving the first couple, Adam and Eve. Instead, Genesis 1–3 should be read as an analysis of the present. The image of God is true of us all—all the time. Even the most hardened criminal still has the capacity to express their better self. And the Fall is also true of us all—all of the time. The symbolism of the Adam and Eve story is that there are propensities inside us that are destructive. We cannot help being selfish (even when we would rather not do so). We cannot help being moody (even when we know we are spoiling the moment). Living close to others is hard. And from time to time, we can be shockingly cruel, whether it takes the form of unkind gossip or wanton and destructive violence.

Christians believe that much of our suffering is due to a conflict between these two competing forces—the image and the fall (notice how we are reintroducing some of the head response to the problem of suffering). Considerable suffering arises from the challenge of learning how to give and receive love. We find ourselves believing that it is fun being part of a tribe that is cruel to outsiders or that we need to be strong by being mean. And in so doing, we find ourselves as part of the processes that cause so much suffering.

Now if the Christian analysis stopped there, then we would be in a very depressing place. However, the good news (literally the "gospel") is that this is the start of the analysis that gets much better. The second area is the doctrine of the atonement. This is the extraordinary claim that in some mysterious sense the God-man who died on the cross provides the means to the redemption of the world.

The idea that the death of Jesus has made it possible for our relationship with each other and with God to be transformed is at the heart of the New Testament witness. In Mark's gospel, we find the image of ransom occurring: "For the Son of Man came not to be served but to serve, and to give his life a ransom for many" (Mark 10:45). In Romans 5:8, the apostle Paul explains: "But God shows his love for us in that while we were yet sinners Christ died for us." Somehow and in some way, the death of Jesus changed our relationship with God.

Most of us find it hard to be agents of love. So the idea that somehow God has done the work in Christ is good news. The thought that we are simply called to "try and try again to be better"— like endless New Year's resolutions—is depressing. Instead all we must do is accept that God has done the hard work of transforming our lives, thereby enabling love to become the dominant theme.

But why should a man dying two thousand years ago have such an impact? The New Testament witness offers a variety of metaphors. We have the image of sacrifice—Jesus is in some sense our sacrifice for sin (Heb. 10:11–13); we have the image of ransom that Christ pays the debt that we owe that then sets us free (Mark 10:45); we have the image of Christ as a victor against the forces of evil (1 John 3:8); and we have the image of Christ as a moral example of a person dying to self that we all should imitate (1 Cor. 1:11). Now the way to read these metaphors is not to commit to any particular image and make it definitive, but to allow all the metaphors to combine to point to the reality beyond the images.

One helpful way to think of the atonement is found in the work of Vernon White. White's starting point is the mystery of forgiveness. It has always been a puzzle why a third party can forgive sins. If John hurts Peter, then how can it help for John to ask Joan for forgiveness? How can any third party, whether it is Joan or God, forgive on behalf of the wronged party? White gives an interesting answer: the only way that perhaps divine forgiveness could work is if God has been a victim of wickedness and if God in a very real sense touches every aspect of tragedy in creation.

Given that Jesus is God, the suffering of Jesus is unique. The suffering is both the creator who is in everything and everywhere and also an individual person. In being tortured to death as a human, the Creator is then able to bring about restoration and reconciliation in the creation. Perhaps a possible parallel is the suffering of Nelson Mandela. In much the same way as his suffering (the twenty-seven years in prison—the best years of his adult life) made his calls for the black man to love (and therefore forgive) his white oppressor "morally authentic," so God has the same authenticity by virtue of the suffering of Jesus.

The idea of the atonement has real power in three ways. First, we learn of the seriousness that God takes the reality of evil and suffering. We have seen that the Christian faith does not explain *why* evil is permitted, but the fact that God had to endure suffering and pain (the cost to God is high) strongly suggests that the reason for evil and suffering must be a very good one. Given that God had to suffer, then God must have thought long and hard (please permit the anthropomorphic image) and determined that suffering and evil were indeed inescapable.

Second, as we saw in the earlier chapter, the fact that the Creator hangs on the cross is the ultimate recognition of God taking responsibility for the hurt and pain in the creation. God is ultimately responsible for the creation: therefore, God is ultimately responsible for the suffering of innocent children. In the tradition of "anger against God," which is found in the Psalms, sometimes in our anger and despair at the evil in this world, we need to see God suffer. Sometimes we need to see the cross as God getting God's just desserts for the hellish lives that millions of people are living. Acknowledging a legitimate anger against God is an aspect of the cross.

31

Third, we can now see how Jesus makes restoration possible because Jesus enables God to forgive. Suffering brings a certain moral authority and entitlement. Going back to Nelson Mandela for a moment, it is the fact he suffered that gave him the authority to inspire and forgive on behalf of others who suffered. Mandela wrote:

> I knew that people expected me to harbor anger towards whites. But I had none. In prison, my anger towards whites decreased, but my hatred for the system grew. I wanted South Africa to see that I loved even my enemies while I hated the system that turned us against one another.[1]

Mandela had as many reasons as anyone to hate the white oppressor. And it is because he had suffered at the hands of the white man that his calls to "love" the white man became all the more powerful. His suffering had given him the authority to reassure the white man that they could be forgiven and were still welcome in a multiracial South Africa. With God, the authority is total: God both suffers directly in Jesus and indirectly in every instance of pain and injustice in creation. By virtue of this combination, God through Christ has created the conditions for us to be restored.

Through the pivotal movement of repentance, the action of God in Christ gives God the authority to forgive those moments when egoism, selfishness, and hatred dominate, thereby affording an opportunity to live a life open to the transforming power of God's love. In other words, an important part of the Christian response to suffering is that we accept the invitation of God to

---

[1] Nelson Mandela, *Long Walk to Freedom* (London: Abacus, 1994), 680.

allow grace to overcome our propensity to evil and allow love to then dominate.

We turn now to the third aspect of the wider Christian narrative that illuminates the problem of suffering. Our struggle for transformation is not an isolated challenge, but rather should take place within a mutually supporting community. This is where our ecclesiology (our view of the church) comes in. The church is not simply another organization, but an agent of divine transformation. The church is not just an hour on Sunday morning, but a Spirit-led community that is called to transform individuals and the world.

One important part of the Christian response to suffering is that we, ourselves, are supposed to be part of the solution. To use technical language, this is the work of the Holy Spirit within the context of the church. The Holy Spirit is the aspect of God that connects to our lives. So the power of God that is enabled through the cross to transform lives is implemented through the Holy Spirit, and the church is the community in which the Holy Spirit works. On a practical level, this means that as we open our lives to the agency of divine love, we find our propensities to be unkind and inconsiderate dissipating and our desires to help others increasing. This, at least, is the theory; in practice, religious people can often add to suffering instead of reducing it. But ideally, the church is the space from which women and men emerge to take part in decreasing the amount of suffering in the world.

The final aspect is our eschatological hope (eschatology means "doctrines about the end"), which invites us to place the struggles of human existence into an appropriate context. It is difficult to make sense of suffering if this life is all there is. Too many lives are brutally curtailed—the illness that takes a child; the teenager who is compelled to become part of an army and then killed in a raid;

and the innocent bystander who dies from a suicide bomber while having dinner out with friends. It was the great European philosopher Immanuel Kant who insisted that the justice of the universe requires life beyond the grave. One cannot believe that ultimately the universe is fair and just without this larger context.

As a result, a major part of the Christian response to suffering is the simple affirmation of eternal life. This does not mean that we are promised a "pie in the sky," but rather that we are invited to place this moment of human existence into the context of eternity. So as individuals we will die, and as a planet and a species, our time on earth will come to an end. These realities invite us to participate in the promise of an ultimate reconciliation in the cosmos between the injustices we have suffered and the love we have been promised.

But is this plausible? The starting point when thinking about life beyond the grave is to think about the miracle of life now. There is something amazing about the simple gift of "being." We breathe, think, and enjoy a rich visual, sensual experience of the world. It is all so mysterious. Although science provides real insight into the miracle of being, this actually heightens our awe in much the same way that knowing how to read sheet music heightens one sense of awe at the remarkable experience of listening to Pachelbel's canon in D major.

The sense of awe feeds on the spiritual dimension of living. As we marvel, we slowly appreciate that the material is only part of everything that is. There is, in everything, a sense of transcendence that can be seen through the material. In the same way as the imaginative life of the mind cannot be seen as the surgeon operates on the brain, so the spiritual depths of reality transcend the immediate animal, plant, and mineral categories of life. Once one sees that there is more to this life than the material now, then one can see how there will be more to this life in future.

The Christian claim for life after death is found in the resurrection of Jesus. The biblical witness teaches that, much to the surprise of the disciples, the crucified Jesus did not stay in the tomb. Jesus became the "first born" (Rev. 1:4) of all of us. In the resurrection appearances of the Gospels, we see some continuities (Jesus is recognized by the disciples and can eat food), yet there are some differences (Jesus can move through a closed door). So from the resurrection of Jesus, we arrive at the following account of life beyond the grave. It seems we will have a mental life located within a body, what the apostle Paul saw as a transformed self. The precise nature of the body is difficult to describe. But Paul seems to see it like this: just as there is a different flesh for animals and humans, so there will be different bodies for earth and heaven (see 1 Cor. 15:39). It seems then that we will have an individual body that will operate significantly differently from our present one. Presumably we will need some sort of space/time framework (it is difficult to see how bodies could operate without such), but courtesy of perhaps teleporting or telepathy, we will not be subject to the restrictions that we currently endure. We will be recognizable (as Jesus was to his disciples) and will meet up with those we love.

The *why suffering* question needs to be located in this wider Christian narrative. As we do so, we can see how the challenge of suffering is all part of the divine project of teaching us how to give and receive love. We can see how we all have potential for great good because of the image and for great evil because of the fall. We can also see how God gets involved in the tragedy of suffering. God lives among us and dies as a common criminal. In the death of Jesus, God creates a power that enables God to forgive everything in our past and invites us to join a community that is being slowly transformed by the agency of the Spirit. And we are promised in the resurrection of Jesus that ultimately we will be freed from this realm where we are just learning to love and invited into a realm where love has already triumphed.

None of this explains suffering. But it does offer rich and deep perspectives on the nature of suffering and how suffering should be understood. The next challenge is to learn to cope with suffering. And this is the work of the last chapter.

5

Coping with Suffering

Every single person suffers. It is inescapable. It takes a variety of forms. At the most obvious, we have the suffering of illness and death. We are all going to die. And we are all going to die because of something. So at some point in our lives, it is likely that our aging body will find it hard to run or walk or, even more practically, pick up an object that has fallen on the floor. Many of us will find ourselves coping with a stroke or cancer or a heart attack. And physical suffering is only the start.

Such are the complexities of living; all of us, at one time or another, will cope with the pain of human relationships. We will love another who will not love us back. Many people are in unhappy marriages that cause day-to-day suffering, and others are desperate to be married and are coping with long, lonely evenings by themselves. We might find ourselves marginalized on an edge of a group. We might find ourselves the target of prejudice. It might be loneliness, vulnerability, or neglect. More seriously, it might be bullying or abuse.

Then we have the suffering of activity. A typical life (assuming we make 80 years) only has 29,200 days. It is amazing the number of people who are spending a large number of those days in work that they hate. It might be a toxic work environment, it might be boring, or it might be a long commute. There are women and men who are coping with the disappointment of not doing well at school or being passed over for promotion.

Then we have the irritations of life. Sitting in a traffic queue or getting frustrated as a flight is cancelled—these are moments that fill one with gloom and anger. Other irritations include forgetting your password to get into an account or trying to explain to the cable company on the phone that "yes, you are sure the cable is not working, despite their impression." It is not unusual for people to scream and shout at such moments. These four areas—physical, relational, activity, and irritations—are the visible side of suffering.

But then there is the suffering of the interior life. The person who cannot admit to themselves, let alone to others, their feelings of same-sex attraction. The harried business person who cannot pass a day without at least a bottle of wine in the evening. Addictions are often the result of some deep internal conflict and can take many forms, from pornography to drugs. The opioids crisis (the addiction to heroin, prescription pain relievers, and fentanyl) is killing over ninety Americans every day; this crisis is costing America over $78.5 billion a year.[1] And, of course, the most serious is the mysterious, difficult world of anxiety disorders and depression. Approximately 18 percent of American adults are suffering from anxiety disorders (thereby making it the most common mental illness in America) and almost 7 percent suffer from depression.[2] Unlike the cancer victim (where others

---

[1] "Opioid Crisis," *National Institute of Drug Abuse*, accessed July 23, 2017, https://www.drugabuse.gov/drugs-abuse/opioids/opioid-crisis.

[2] "Depression," *Anxiety and Depression Association of America*, accessed July 23, 2017, https://adaa.org/understanding-anxiety/depression.

understand why they might be finding life difficult), sufferers of depression have to handle the endless questions like "why can't you just cheer up?" The lack of understanding of depression adds to the extent and depth of their suffering.

Finally, the ripples of suffering are vast. When there is a traffic accident, due perhaps to drinking and driving, and the passenger dies, there is a vast circle of human lives that have to cope with the pain of that moment. For the driver, there is a spouse, children, and parents who are watching a loved one go through the justice system, facing imprisonment, losing her or his job, perhaps losing their home, and coping with the sudden changed circumstances. For the passenger, there are parents, spouses, and children who are all mourning a massive gap in their lives. The new normal in both cases is very hard.

So how do we cope with suffering? In this book, we have grappled with the head responses to suffering, we have felt the heart responses, and we have seen how the entire narrative of faith is an invitation to be aware of the sources of suffering and the resources in God to transform situations of suffering. Now let us get very practical. What are the biblical resources available to help us cope with suffering on a day-to-day basis?

The heart of the biblical response is to invite us to cultivate a certain set of dispositions. We need to learn a sense of gratitude, we need to learn not to worry, and we need to learn to trust the God we believe in. We start with gratitude.

Gratitude

We have already noted that discipleship in the first century could very easily carry a death sentence. Joining the Jesus Movement carried real risks. Most of the disciples were killed by the authorities. In addition to this reality, life in general was very hard. Christianity was mainly an urban religion, and as Rodney Stark explains, urban life in the first century was very hard. He takes Antioch as representative:

> Any accurate portrait of Antioch in New Testament times must depict a city filled with misery, danger, fear, despair, and hatred. A city where the average family lived a squalid life in filthy and cramped quarters, where at least half of the children died at birth or during infancy, and where most of the children who lived lost at least one parent before reaching maturity. A city filled with hatred and fear rooted in intense ethnic antagonisms and exacerbated by a constant stream of strangers. A city so lacking in stable networks of attachments that petty incidents could prompt mob violence. A city where crime flourished and the streets were dangerous at night. And, perhaps above all, a city repeatedly smashed by cataclysmic catastrophes: where a resident could expect literally to be homeless from time to time, providing that he or she was among the survivors.[3]

The average life expectancy was probably less than thirty years, and everyone lived with chronic health conditions, mainly due to the lack of effective sanitation and hygiene. The norm was a life in pain. Therefore, there is something amazing about Paul's instructions in Thessalonians.

> See that none of you repays evil for evil, but always seek to do good to one another and to all. Rejoice always, pray without ceasing, give thanks in all circumstances; for this is the will of God in Christ Jesus for you. (1 Thess. 5:15–18)

---

[3] Rodney Stark, *The Rise of Christianity* (San Francisco: Harper, 1997), 160–161.

"Giving thanks in all circumstances" means give thanks in a situation where you are unlikely to live very long, you have already seen those you love die, and you are living in perpetual pain and discomfort.

But there is an important principle here. For Christians, appreciating the gift-like quality of each day is an obligation. If we are breathing, then we have something to be grateful for. It is an invitation to look at living in a certain way. Instead of focusing on all those things we do not have (the perfect job, the perfect partner, the perfect vacation, or the perfect car), we should focus on the many things we do have (sight, hearing, friends, food, a home, and a new day).

From outside the circle of faith, the religious capacity for "giving thanks" is puzzling. You will often hear a devout Christian say, "we were in an accident with the entire car written off and all the passengers had broken bones, but we are grateful to God for the fact that we all survived." If God gets the credit for those surviving, then why doesn't God get the blame for the initial accident?

And herein is an important truth about Christianity. Christians are very aware of the tragic. The focus of our liturgy is a young man dying at the hands of the Roman Empire. Yet we both see the tragic and are grateful for the tragic. (In the Eucharist, the prayer of consecration of the bread and the wine is called the Great Thanksgiving.) In Jesus, we can see the tragic, yet we believe that in that tragedy is the redemption of the world.

But there is more. Christians should not assume that life is always going to be good. It is strange, but many people only realize how much they have when they lose it. They are only grateful for good health when they are undergoing treatment for cancer. Christians believe it is essential to be grateful for all the good things we have while we have them. And yes, if we do lose

41

that good thing (say our eyesight), we are called to be grateful for the fact that "at least we had good sight for so long." Learning a disposition of gratitude means that we learn that the normal is great and the normal might not always be.

It is Alain De Botton, a contemporary atheist secularist, who actually appreciates this side of religion. He writes:

> One of the differences between religious and secular lives is that in the former, one says thank you all the time: when eating, going to bed, waking up etc.
>
> Why does the secular world tend not to say thank you? At the most obvious level, there seems no one to say thank you to. But, more importantly, offering thanks for relatively minor aspects of life risks appearing unambitious and undignified. The sort of things for which our ancestors bowed down, we pride ourselves on having done enough work to take for granted. Would we really need to pause for a moment of gratitude at the oily darkness of a handful of olives or at the fragrant mottled skin of a lemon? Are there not greater goals towards which we might be aiming?
>
> In our refusal, we are attempting to flee a sense of vulnerability. We do not say thank you for a sunset because we think there will be many more—and because we assume there must be more exciting things to look forward to. To feel grateful is to allow oneself to sense how much one is at the mercy of events. It is to accept that there may come a point when our extraordinary plans for ourselves have run aground, our horizons have narrowed and we have nothing more opulent to wonder at than the sight of a bluebell or a clear evening sky. To say thank you for a glass of wine or a piece of cheese is a kind of preparation for death, for the modesty that our dying days will demand.
>
> That's why, even in a secular life, we should make space for some thank yous to no one in particular. A person who remembers to be

grateful is more aware of the role of gifts and luck—and so readier to meet with the tragedies that are awaiting us all down the road.[4]

It is all a question of perspective. Learning to express gratitude for everything helps us cope with the inevitable challenges and pain of living.

Do not worry

We started this chapter listing the many ways in which we can suffer. There is a sense in which life is precarious and fragile. As a result, many of us can spend a significant percentage of any day feeling "anxious." This anxiety, this worry, means that we stop focusing on the moment and instead focus on what might happen. We worry about the test the doctor wants to do, we worry about whether we can pay our bills this month, we worry about the teenage children on a road trip together, we worry about our marriage, and we worry about whether we will keep our job; in short, we worry about everything.

Jesus is completely clear. We are commanded not to worry. It is debilitating, damaging, and an act of unfaithfulness. Jesus explains:

> Therefore I tell you, do not worry about your life, what you will eat or what you will drink, or about your body, what you will wear. Is not life more than food, and the body more than clothing? Look at the birds of the air; they neither sow nor reap

---

[4] Alain De Botton, "Ideas for Modern Living: Gratitude," *The Guardian*, March 13, 2010. Accessed July 25, 2017, https://www.theguardian.com/lifeandstyle/2010/mar/14/alain-botton-ideas-modern-living-gratitude.

nor gather into barns, and yet your heavenly Father feeds them. Are you not of more value than they? And can any of you by worrying add a single hour to your span of life? And why do you worry about clothing? Consider the lilies of the field, how they grow; they neither toil nor spin, yet I tell you, even Solomon in all his glory was not clothed like one of these. But if God so clothes the grass of the field, which is alive today and tomorrow is thrown into the oven, will he not much more clothe you—you of little faith? Therefore do not worry, saying, "What will we eat?" or "What will we drink?" or "What will we wear?" For it is the Gentiles who strive for all these things; and indeed your heavenly Father knows that you need all these things. But strive first for the kingdom of God and his righteousness, and all these things will be given to you as well. So do not worry about tomorrow, for tomorrow will bring worries of its own. Today's trouble is enough for today.

Matt. 6:25–34

Here Jesus is explaining that worry is wrong for a whole host of reasons. First, he points out that worry is futile. You don't add a "single hour" to your life span by worrying. Worry makes no constructive difference. Nothing is going to change because you laid awake at night worrying about something. Second, we need faith and trust in the moment. A person of faith needs to surrender their life to God. And in so doing, we need to relax and enjoy that we are blessed with a friendship with the Creator of the Universe. For a person of faith, there is no scenario that doesn't ultimately result in hopefulness and joy. The death of a loved one can be excruciating, but slowly we will struggle and learn that the loved one truly is in the hands of God. When we see the vast canvas that God is working on, we are invited to trust that the picture God is painting with our lives will be good. We will, of course, still suffer. But we surrender our concern about fearful possibilities and trust instead in the God who loves us. Third, focus on the moment. There is some humor in Jesus' concluding remarks. Jesus seems to be saying that we have enough problems right now; there is no need for us to spend time anticipating potential difficulties tomorrow.

Most of the things that we worry about are not realized. So it is a wasted energy. One exercise that counsellors suggest for people who worry is to write down their worry and put it in a "worry jar." At the end of the week, they then empty the worry jar and note how many of their fears for the future were not realized. We may worry about a meeting, a trip, or a visit to the doctor, and at the end of the week, we realize that none of our worries came to be. It was all a complete waste of time.

The wisdom in the counsel of Jesus is considerable. The Gospel invitation is to live in the moment. Enjoy the day. Enjoy the flower, the sunlight in the trees, the beauty of an old building, the children, and the meal one is about to eat. The result is that one lives deeply in the presence.

Finally, let us concede it is hard. Worrying comes so naturally. And even if intellectually we are persuaded by the wisdom of Jesus, it is hard to live. So the advice of the apostle Paul in Philippians is helpful at this point. He wrote, "Do not worry about anything, but in everything by prayer and supplication with thanksgiving let your requests be made known to God. And the peace of God, which surpasses all understanding, will guard your hearts and your minds in Christ Jesus" (Phil. 4:6). According to Paul, there are three steps:

1 Do not worry.
2 Turn every worry into a prayer.
3 Then let the peace of God descend upon you.

Instead of worrying, we pray. We take the worry and give it over to God. And then as a result, we can be sure that the peace of Christ will descend upon us.

Trust

So much suffering is less about what happens to us and more about how we react to what happens to us. You inadvertently reverse a car into a street light pole. The dent is significant, as will be the cost of the repair. Now you can react in one of two ways to this moment. First, you can start with a variety of expletives. Perhaps allow the problem to cast a big shadow over the day. Insist on several drinks, yell at the kids, and generally stomp around the house for several days. Second, you can and should be disappointed in your driving, but then let the disappointment stop there. You will recognize that the cost of repair will have to be found somewhere, but apart from that you will try and place the problem in context. It is just a car. It is just a dent. The children are safe; the home is still there; and you can go and have a cup of tea, after all, the car is still drivable.

The second reaction is much more sensible. It is a reaction that doesn't make the situation worse. It places the problem in context; it celebrates so much that one should be grateful for. The first reaction makes the problem much harder, while the second reaction trusts that the problem can be overcome.

The act of trusting is a fundamental biblical theme. It is found preeminently in the Psalter—that remarkable collection of hymn-like compositions right at the heart of Scripture. The idea of trusting is found in the context of pain and suffering. Two illustrations will suffice, both of which are psalms of lament. In Psalm 9, the context is struggles with enemies (both the enemies of the Lord and the enemies of the author). The end of the psalm concludes with this exhortation:

> The Lord is a stronghold for the oppressed,
>   a stronghold in times of trouble.
> And those who know your name put their trust in you,
>   for you, O Lord, have not forsaken those who seek you.
>
> Ps. 9:9–10

For the author, the human realm was full of evil forces; the author was feeling isolated and afraid. But then the author recognized that God will not forsake those who trust God. The very act of making ourselves open to God (in the act of trust) gives God the space to strengthen and protect. This is because God respects human free will (back to one of those head responses in chapter two). And a life that opens to God in an act of trust creates space in that life for God to help and shape our responses to the challenges.

A second psalm of lament is Psalm 13. In this case, the author was feeling neglected and ignored by God. The psalm starts with "How long, O Lord? Will you forget me for ever?" The author was worried about dying: "Consider and answer me, O Lord my God! Give light to my eyes, or I will sleep the sleep of death" (v. 3). But the psalm concludes:

> But I trusted in your steadfast love;
>   my heart shall rejoice in your salvation.
> I will sing to the Lord,
>   because he has dealt bountifully with me.
>
> Ps. 13:5–6

The act of trust for the psalmist involved a refocusing. Instead of concentrating on the immediate, local, and (yes) major problems, the act of trust shifts the focus to the eternal and the cosmic.

It is all a matter of horizons. Sometimes our horizon is just our lives with the immediate problems. But the act of trust shifts one's eyes around from our lives to the horizon of the creator God. Suddenly we see things more clearly.

Perspective is often a crucial factor in coping with suffering. Our disappointment that our vacation has been cancelled is real. But if one shifts focus from that disappointment to the many remarkable features of our lives that are good, then suddenly our disappointment matters less. When we look away from the disappointment and focus on our health, our friends, and our home, the disappointment is reduced in size. And when we locate our disappointment in the life of the Creator God—the Creator responsible for the billions of people on earth and probably other life forms on other planets—then our disappointment becomes utterly trivial.

Now of course missing a vacation is a relatively small moment of suffering. Suffering takes many forms, and, of course, disappointment about anything is a relatively trivial form. But this is where the Psalms have a point. Even a major form of suffering (where you are being attacked by enemies and could be murdered) is still very small when located in the life of God and in the perspective of eternity. Suffering is seen differently when the perspective of divine agency within the cosmos. Stars have formed and died; dinosaurs have arrived and left; earthquakes, fires, and floods, which are now distance memories, have destroyed cities. The God we worship is the God of the entire cosmos, all of history, and everything that now is. This act of locating even the tragic in the life of God provides a new context that changes the way we look at our problems.

Conclusion

So why suffering? A neat answer is not available. It is not like the question, why is there water coming through the ceiling of my apartment? There is no equivalent for the plumber who can explain that the water pipe has burst in the bathroom. In the world of God-discourse (the technical meaning of the word "theology"), we create a picture that seeks to illuminate the ultimate mystery of the divine intention.

The picture painted in this book focuses on the witness of Scripture. The Bible is silent when it comes to a rational explanation for the "why" of suffering. Indeed, Job is very clear: this is not available. Yet the Bible is deeply illuminating as to the mechanics of suffering. God embarked on a "love project" in creation. Humans are called to discover love, but that is hard because we enjoy the opposite (being selfish, cruel, unkind, a gossip, and so forth) so much. Out of love, God has revealed his nature in Christ. In the Incarnation we see God participating in and embracing the suffering of the world. We are also invited to seize the gift of a forgiven life made possible by the death of Jesus. We then become part of a community, the church, which strives to allow the agency of God to transform our lives and make us more open to the spirit of love. And finally, in the greater cosmic scheme, we know that all suffering is redeemed through participation in the resurrected divine life made possible by Christ. In addition, there are biblical resources that help us cope with suffering. We are invited to learn to be grateful, we are forbidden to worry, and we are called to trust. These three acts can provide a transformative focus on the challenges of suffering.

But is this sufficient? Does this focus on the mechanics of suffering really provide a reason for suffering? I can understand if a reader finds this completely inadequate. We would all prefer the clarity of the plumber. And it is interesting how the "head answer" that focused on human free will has emerged in later chapters. One can see how a world like this is necessary for the emergence of humans who are called to learn how to give and receive love. One can see how genuine human freedom is a condition for God's "love project." So although these answers feel inadequate, they do actually make sense.

Yet, I return to Good Friday. It is this moment that provides the response of most power. Good Friday is rightly acclaimed as the most serious and solemn day in the Church calendar. It is difficult to fathom everything that was going on that day. But the eyes of faith see God at that moment hanging on the cross. And along with God, we can see every refugee, every damaged child, every mom afraid that this test might show cancer, and every victim of a drunk driver. In fact, every instance of suffering in creation is captured in that moment when Jesus Christ, the Incarnation of God, died on a cross just outside Jerusalem.